THE F[image_ref id="1" /]TO

NATURE

Animals, Plants and Birds in
Southwest Ontario from Toronto to Windsor

Written and illustrated by

Form   Limited

To Simeon Cochrane:
Enjoy the wildlife around you and draw from it.
— Uncle Jeff

Formac Publishing Company Limited acknowledges the support of the cultural affairs section, Nova Scotia Department of Tourism, Culture and Heritage. We acknowledge the financial support of the Government of Canada through the Book Publishing Industry Development Program (BPIDP) for our publishing activities. We acknowledge the support of the Canada Council for the Arts for our publishing program.

Library and Archives Canada Cataloguing in Publication

Domm, Jeffrey C., 1958-
    Formac pocketguide to nature : animals, plants and birds in southwest Ontario from Toronto to Windsor / written & illustrated by Jeffrey C. Domm.

Includes index.
ISBN 0-88780-661-9

      1. Animals—Ontario, Southwestern—Identification. 2. Plants—
Ontario, Southwestern—Identification. 3. Birds—Ontario,
Southwestern—Identification. 4. Natural history—Ontario,
Southwestern—Guidebooks.
I. Title. II. Title: Pocketguide to nature.

QH106.2.O5D65 2005   578'.09713'2   C2005-901668-X

Formac Publishing Company Limited
5502 Atlantic Street
Halifax, Nova Scotia
B3H 1G4
www.formac.ca

Printed and bound in China

Photo credits
Pages 4 and 7, Don Lounder;
page 5, Vineland Estates
Winery; page 6, Dwayne Coon.

Table of Contents

Preface

In southwest Ontario there is an abundance of
diverse nature hotspots, all of which can be
reached by a network of highways and back roads.

In early spring, birders flock to Point Pelee and
Longpoint to greet the influx of migrating
songbirds. At the same time, throughout the
hardwood forests along the Bruce Trail, the forest
floor is coming back to life with wildflowers and
salamander breeding ponds. In summer the beach
areas of Presqu'ile, Sandbanks and Pinery
provincial parks offer interpretive hiking trails, and
in protected areas around Rondeau and Pelee
there are special opportunities to see butterflies
that are very rare in the rest of Ontario. In the fall,
the brilliance of colour in the forest is an invitation
to walkers, and as November approaches, deer
become more visible in many rural areas. In
winter, on the Sauble's cross-country ski trails,

aspiring naturalists can follow the tracks of foxes and coyotes in their search for mice and voles living just under the cover of snow.

This guide will assist you in your quest to enjoy the outdoors and understand more about what you see there. This portable pocket guide, designed for nature lovers of all ages, covers the most commonly encountered species for each life form — animals, insects, plants and trees. Along with the illustration and description of each species, useful sighting tips are included in order to enhance both your identification and knowledge of interesting species.  Keep an eye open to the habitats and seasons sections. Often times it is these little bits of information that will help you to make that final identification.

Gordon Lewer
Hamilton, Ontario
March 2005

Introduction

Ordinary events in the natural world can be astonishing when we see them for the first time. The hatching of hundreds of spiders from their tiny ball of white fluff, or the sight of an osprey hovering in the sky, watching for the moment to

drop into the water to catch its prey— these are events that make us inquisitive about the creatures and plants with which we share the planet. Questions come up that need answers.

In this book you will find helpful information about animals, insects and plants that you are most likely to see in your community, both in your very own back yard and in the parks, woodlands and fields nearby. Each chapter of the book gives the top-ten species you are most likely to see in each category. For example, in the mammals section, there is a page on the raccoon and one on the white-tailed deer. These species, quite familiar to many of us, are followed by other species that can also be seen in the wild, but less frequently.

Enjoying the beauty of nature is a means for many of us to escape from the noise and agitation of our everyday lives. We find peace and inspiration by spending time in a forest or beside a lake. Some people prefer woodland to

prairie grassland, and some people like to explore rivers and lakes. Others cannot resist the call of hills and mountains. You may be more interested in trees than insects, or prefer to watch birds over butterflies. Whatever your preference, when you spend time observing the creatures and plants in the wild, you will see your curiosity grow with each new phenomenon.

You may turn over a decaying log to discover a world of living organisms that scamper off to avoid the light. In the meadow grass you will see insects, butterflies and wildflowers, and if you are really quiet, you might notice a slight rustle and a quick movement out of the corner of your eye, and you will see the tail of a snake as it slithers under cover. Quiet contemplation on a riverbank might bear witness to a beaver, muskrat or turtle swimming by.

As you use this guide in your nature walks, you will gather a greater respect for the interdependency of everything in all ecosystems.

Everything in nature has its preferred habitats. Preserving these habitats is very important to maintain the balance of nature.

Naturalists take notes and photographs, and endeavour never to take anything out of its habitat. And the only thing they leave behind are footprints.

How to Use This Book

When you encounter wildlife you will consider size, colour, behaviour, season, location and sounds. This book gives you a simple and visual way to identify the species, and uses text only where necessary.

Understanding the Symbols

Habitats

These symbols identify the kinds of ecosystems that you will encounter on your walk. Some species are found in only one habitat, others in several.

 Garden

 Lake

 Farmland

 Marsh

 Forest

 Meadow

 Industrial Area

Size

Smaller species are compared to an adult human hand that is 15 cm (6 in) from wrist to tip of middle finger. Larger species are compared to a 1.8 m (6 ft) human form, and still larger ones, such as trees, are compared to a house that is 12 m (40 ft) tall.

Magnifying Glass

 These tiny species are best observed with a magnifying glass.

Flying Patterns

 Quick wingbeats

 Slow steady wingbeats

 Soaring

 Wingbeats followed by gliding

Warning Symbol

 Poisonous! Do not touch!

Tree Symbols

 One half of this symbol shows the tree as it appears in the winter (bare), and the other half shows how it appears in the summer (complete foliage).

Mammals

Mammals are vertebrate animals with hair on their bodies. Their young are alive at birth and they are nourished by milk from their mother. Often small and helpless in the early days of life, young mammals develop slowly, and take a long time to reach adulthood. Mammals are often very adaptable. Their body temperature is regulated according to the environment, and having hair of various thicknesses for protection allows them to survive in varying climates and different habitats.

Size and colour are the first clues to identifying a mammal. Other outstanding characteristics include the shape of its head, including ears and snout, the length of its tail and speed of movement.

Many mammals that survive well in areas of human habitation move around at night. Foxes, bats and raccoons are more apt to be nocturnal, and you will see and hear them during late evening walks.

Several of the larger species identified in this book will attack other mammals such as humans and dogs when their young are approached. Always give these animals plenty of room and observe from a distance.

White-tailed Deer
Odocoileus virginianus

Size

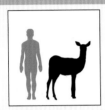

Habitat

Sound

Hoofbeats can be heard in the distance when bounding.

- Red-brown overall, grey in winter
- Males have antlers up to 90 cm (36 in) across
- White fur inside ears, on belly, on underside of tail and circling around the eyes
- Fawns are light red-brown with white spots

BEHAVIOUR

Most active in early morning and evening. Tail is held erect when running, revealing white underside.

Observation Calendar
J F M A M J J A S O N D

12

Raccoon
Procyon lotor

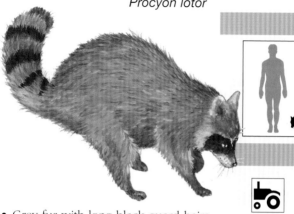

Size

Habitat

- Grey fur with long black guard hairs
- Large, bushy tail with 4 to 6 black bands
- Distinctive black mask on face
- Small, dexterous, human-like hands with claws

BEHAVIOUR
Generally slow-moving but can run fast when frightened. Inquisitive and will approach if food is detected.

DID YOU KNOW?
Raccoons build nests inside hollow trees which they line with leaves. Litters of young range from 1 to 8 kits.

Observation Calendar

J F M A M J J A S O N D

Red Fox
Vulpes vulpes

Size

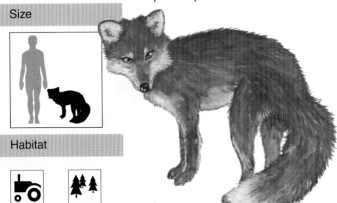

Habitat

- Red-brown overall with darker brown feet and white underbelly
- Long, bushy tail with white tip
- Erect pointed ears, black on outside
- Overall colour variations include black, silver grey, and mixed

Sound

Unlike wolves or coyotes, foxes don't call out often. They have a shrill barking yelp.

BEHAVIOUR

Very secretive and shy, mostly nocturnal.

DID YOU KNOW?

The Red Fox has the largest geographical range of any carnivore now present in North America.

Observation Calendar
J F M A M J J A S O N D

Muskrat
Ondatra zibethicus

Size

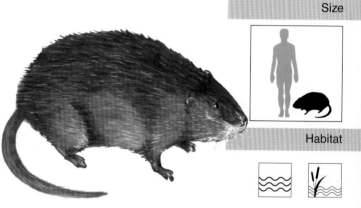

Habitat

- Roundish body with dark brown and black fur
- Appears similar to beaver but tail is much thinner
- White fur around the mouth
- Small, black eyes and small ears

DID YOU KNOW?
Muskrats build lodges similar to the beaver's but on a smaller scale. They do not construct dams.

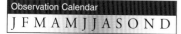

Observation Calendar

J F M A M J J A S O N D

Meadow Jumping Mouse
Zapus hudsonius

Size

Habitat

- Brown above with yellowish sides and white belly
- Tiny, white front paws and longer back paws
- Long tail with white tip

BEHAVIOUR

Quick movements, mostly jumping from one location to another.

DID YOU KNOW?

A portion of the Meadow Jumping Mouse's diet is a fungus called Endogone. The consumption and excretion of the fungus helps the fungus to germinate.

Observation Calendar

J F M A M J J A S O N D

Eastern Chipmunk
Tamias striatus

Size

Habitat

- Small and red-brown overall with white belly
- 1 white stripe bordered by 2 black stripes mark each side
- Dark brown and black stripes down back
- Large cheek pouches

BEHAVIOUR

Darts about, pausing frequently to assess its surroundings.

DID YOU KNOW?

Chipmunks hibernate, but can sometimes be seen popping their heads up on warmer winter days.

Sound

Very vocal with high-pitched, repeated chattering.

Observation Calendar

J F M A M J J A S O N D

North American Porcupine
Erithizon dorsatum

Size

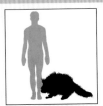

Habitat

- Brown and black overall
- Small eyes against dark face

BEHAVIOUR

Sure-footed and slow moving. Lives in trees, descending to move from one tree to another and to forage.

DID YOU KNOW?

Porcupines cannot shoot their quills at attackers. Instead, they have around 30,000 quills, each lined with barbs that allow the quills to embed easily in flesh that brushes even lightly against them.

Observation Calendar

J F M A M J J A S O N D

18

Woodchuck
Marmota monax

Size

Habitat

- Dark, grizzled, red-brown overall
- Small ears and bushy tail
- Dark brown or black feet

DID YOU KNOW?

Enjoys warm weather and is active mostly in early morning or late afternoon. Can be seen along roadsides moving slowly and occasionally peeking up from its grazing on the short grass.

Observation Calendar

J F M A M J J A S O N D

19

Eastern Grey Squirrel
Sciurus carolinensis

Size

Habitat

Sound

Loud, frenzied chattering when alarmed.

- Light grey overall with buff underbelly
- Red-brown face
- Flat bushy tail

BEHAVIOUR
Most time is spent in trees. Look for large nest at top of tree. Darts about on ground.

DID YOU KNOW?
The Easter Grey Squirrel buries food for winter and can later identify its cache by smell, even under half a metre of snow!

Observation Calendar
J F M A M J J A S O N D

Eastern Cottontail
Sylvilagus floridanus

Size

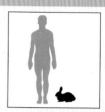

- Greyish brown overall with lighter underbelly, forehead often has white spot
- Long upright ears
- Short, cottony tail
- Rust-coloured nape

Habitat

BEHAVIOUR
Spends most of day grazing in grassy areas near bushes. Jumps quickly when frightened.

Sound

None. Squeals loudly when grabbed by predator.

DID YOU KNOW?
The Cottontail produces litters of 4–5 young, 3–4 times per year. The total offspring produced by 2 rabbits and their descendants could number 350,000 in a 5-year period.

Observation Calendar
J F M A M J J A S O N D

21

Beaver

- Large, wide body with dark brown fur
- Hind feet black, webbed
- Small eyes and ears
- Tail slaps on the water can be heard before a beaver dives. Otherwise beavers are very quiet.

117 cm / 46 in

Striped Skunk

- Black overall with distinctive white stripe running entire length of body
- Thin white line running down face

76 cm / 30 in

Red Squirrel

- Small and red-brown overall with brightest red on sides, white underbelly
- Makes a repeated chattering call similar to chipmunk's but louder and quicker

38 cm / 15 in

Opossum

- Cat-sized, grey and white, grizzled overall
- Long, pink snout
- Makes a loud hissing when alarmed, otherwise silent

80 cm / 32 in

Little Brown Bat

- Red-brown overall with dark wings and ears
- Long, dark-brown wings remain folded when bat is resting
- Call is a very quick *squeak*. Mostly quiet

10 cm / 4 in

Eastern Pipistrelle

- Light brown overall, long, tri-coloured hairs over entire body except for wings
- Large brown ears
- Mostly nocturnal but can be seen just before nightfall in pursuit of flying insects

7.5 cm / 3 in

Reptiles & Amphibians

Reptiles and amphibians are vertebrates, like mammals, but they cannot regulate their body temperature. They bask in the sun to get warm and become active, and they have to cool off in the shade. In cold weather they are sluggish and in winter they hibernate, becoming almost lifeless. Reptiles have scaly skin that keeps their bodies from drying out.

Amphibians are similar to reptiles but they live both on land and in water. The young are hatched from eggs. Young reptiles look like small versions of the adults, but amphibians go through a larval stage. For example, tadpoles are the larval stage of frogs.

With the exception of frogs and turtles, most reptiles and amphibians are secretive and difficult to see. Snakes and salamanders demand close observation strategies by the would-be naturalist since much of their day is spent under decaying trees and rotting debris. None of the reptiles and amphibians in this book are considered venomous or harmful to humans. Some research has shown that the handling of certain reptiles or amphibians has a long term effect on the animal, so it's best to leave them alone.

Eastern American Toad
Bufo americanus americanus

Size

Habitat

Sound

Steady musical trill lasting 20-30 seconds.

- Mottled with grey, brown, tan and black
- Overall "warty" or bumpy skin
- Large gland just behind eyes
- Long toes; middle toe longest

BEHAVIOUR
Small hops, not long jumps. Moves about slowly and heavily.

DID YOU KNOW?
Folklore wrongly warns that if you touch a toad you will get warts. The toad's "warts" are glands with secretions that protect it from predator bites.

Observation Calendar
J F M A M J J A S O N D

Bullfrog
Rana catesbeiana

Size

Habitat

- Dark olive and green, sometimes brown
- Head is green changing to green-yellow behind neck
- Yellow throat in males, white in females
- Tympanic (ear) membrane larger than eye in males

Sound

Low booming call with three beats, sounds like "*jug-o'-rum.*"

BEHAVIOUR
In water, remains still with head just above surface. Jumps suddenly when approached.

DID YOU KNOW?
The Bullfrog is the largest frog in North America. Reaches lengths of 30 cm from nose to toes.

Observation Calendar
J F M A M J J A S O N D

27

Northern Leopard Frog
Rana pipiens

Size

Habitat

Sound

Breeding males make a call that sounds like someone rubbing a wet balloon.

- Green or brown with striking oval-shaped spots
- Long, pointed snout with stripes along sides

BEHAVIOUR
Sits motionless for long periods of time, waiting for prey. Jumps into water when approached.

DID YOU KNOW?
This species has been found in many habitats from forests to deserts to mountain meadows.

Observation Calendar
J F M A M J J A S O N D

Green Frog
Rana clamitans

Size

Habitat

- Colouring variable from green to bronze and brown with mottling
- Yellow chin and underbelly
- Large tympanic (ear) membranes just behind eyes
- Ridges down sides, speckled in brown with small bumps

BEHAVIOUR
Often found warming themselves along muddy shores within a single leap of the water.

DID YOU KNOW?
Green Frogs produce from 1,000 to 5,500 eggs each year.

Sound

Male's breeding call is a loud twang, like the plucking of a banjo string.

Observation Calendar
J F M A M J J A S O N D

29

Eastern Painted Turtle
Chrysemys picta picta

Size

Habitat

- Dark olive and black shell with yellow edges around plates
- Red or orange markings along sides of shell
- Yellow or red stripes along length of neck, yellow markings on head

BEHAVIOUR
Found in ponds and streams with abundant vegetation, sunning in groups on logs or rocks above water. Will dive when approached.

DID YOU KNOW?
The Eastern Painted Turtle hibernates over winter at the bottom of a pond.

Observation Calendar
J F M A M J J A S O N D

30

Eastern Garter Snake

Thamnophis sirtalis sirtalis

Size

Habitat

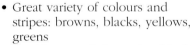

- Great variety of colours and stripes: browns, blacks, yellows, greens
- Double row of alternating black spots between well-defined stripes

BEHAVIOUR

Lies motionless; often found near water.

DID YOU KNOW?

Garter Snakes may strike, or bite when picked up. Though not venomous, they have small teeth that are rarely long enough to puncture skin.

Observation Calendar

J F M A M J J A S O N D

Boreal Chorus Frog
Pseudacris maculata

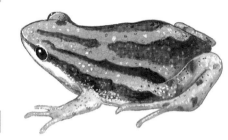

Size

Habitat

Sound

Clicking sound.

- Dark and light stripes along body and head run across eye
- Bands of black and grey on back legs, thighs bright yellow underneath
- Feet have small toe pads

BEHAVIOUR
Nocturnal but occasionally forage in daylight. Though rarely seen they are plentiful, and their chorus of sounds is heard each spring during breeding season.

DID YOU KNOW?
The Boreal Chorus Frog is widespread throughout North America, extending from the Northwest Territories to Texas.

Observation Calendar
J F M A M J J A S O N D

32

Spotted Salamander
Ambystoma maculatum

Size

Habitat

- Dark grey-brown or blue-black overall
- Yellow or orange dots form head to tail
- Long tail tapers to a point
- Ridges run from back to underbelly

BEHAVIOUR

Inconspicuous in day, these nocturnal foragers are busy at night looking for food under ground cover or around logs and rocks where it is moist.

Observation Calendar
J F M A M J J A S O N D

Wood Turtle
Clemmys insculpta

Size

Habitat

- Light brown shell resembles sculpted wood
- Red-orange highlights under chin, on tail and forelegs
- Upper jaw is pointed
- Lighter underside

BEHAVIOUR

Found near water and in moist areas where earthworm populations are high. Hibernates underwater.

DID YOU KNOW?

The Wood Turtle is considered threatened in some parts of Canada.

Observation Calendar
J F M A M J J A S O N D

34

Common Map Turtle
Graptemys geographica

Size

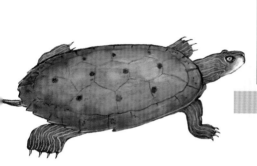

Habitat

- Flat shell, olive, brown or black
- Pale yellow lines on head, legs, neck and tail
- Dark blotches on shell
- Bright yellow eye

BEHAVIOUR
Found in shallow waters where it spends its day hunting for prey.

Observation Calendar
J F M A M J J A S O N D

Northern Spring Peeper

- Tiny frog with large toe pads
- Light brown and grey overall, colouring variable
- Distinctive X pattern on back

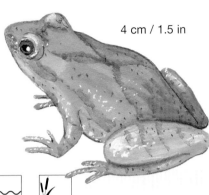

4 cm / 1.5 in

Northern Red-bellied Snake

- Various shades of brown, grey or black on back and sides
- Bright red-orange or orange underbelly
- 3 spots on back of neck

30 cm / 12 in

Wood Frog

8 cm / 3 in

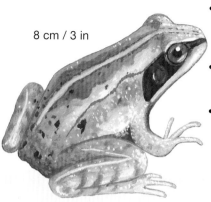

- Greyish brown overall, occasionally tan or red-brown
- Dark mask bordered by cream colour
- Prefers damp areas or ponds within wooded areas

Pickerel Frog

8 cm / 3 in

- Smooth skin with bold dark spots over yellow-brown body
- Small eardrum behind eye
- Makes a steady, low croak

Snapping Turtle

- Large body with flat, dark grey shell mottled with cream colour
- Large claws and feet for digging and swimming
- Large head with hooked jaw
- Long tapered tail

40 cm / 16 in

Northern Brown Snake

- Grey overall, sometimes yellow-brown or red-brown
- Pale underbelly
- Black spots on sides run entire length of body
- Prefers moist areas where it hunts for prey

50 cm / 20 in

Birds

Birds are vertebrates, like
mammals, but their
bone structure is
modified to allow
them to fly. Some of their bones
are hollow, and their front limbs have evolved into
wings. Each bird feather has a centre shaft with
hundreds of side branches, called barbs. Each barb
has two rows of barbules. Feathers trap air, keeping
the bird's weight very low.

There are thousands of species of birds, from the
tiny hummingbird to the huge ostrich. They live in
many different habitats depending on their feeding
needs and their size. Some feed on the ground,
some catch insects in the air and others dive for
their food.

The first clues for identification are colour, size,
call and habitat. Birds can be seen at backyard
feeders, in parks and wilderness areas.

Woodland birds live in trees and bushes, often
close to human habitation. Water birds that nest on
beaches and marshes are very vulnerable to human
disturbance. No matter where you are, if you find a
bird's nest, do not disturb it by touching the eggs or
the young.

Mourning Dove
Zenaida macroura

Size

Habitat

Flying Pattern

Sound

Very distinct cooing that sounds a little sad, *coooahooo-oo-oo-oo* fading at end.

- Buff head and body
- Dark grey wings and tail
- Bill black with speckles of red at opening
- Wings have small black feathers highlighted against softer grey

DID YOU KNOW?

Found in small flocks sitting in rows on telephone wires. Frequent visitor to backyard feeders.

Observation Calendar

J F M A M J J A S O N D

40

Ring-necked Pheasant
Phasianus colchicus

- Male: iridescent green head with distinctive red patches around eyes, white collar; body is grey, black and brown overall with long tail feathers
- Female: buff and brown overall with black mottling
- Both: long tail feathers with black bands

DID YOU KNOW?
Usually found in small groups, especially during mating season.

Observation Calendar
J F M A M J J A S O N D

Size

Habitat

Flying Pattern

Sound

Loud, harsh *uurk-rk*.

Blue Jay
Cyanocitta cristata

Size

Habitat

Flying Pattern

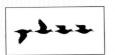

Sound

Call is *jay jay jay*, plus many other calls including the mimicking of hawks.

- Bright blue with black band around the neck
- White chin, cheeks and belly
- Wings and tail blue, banded with black
- Large, black bill pointed

DID YOU KNOW?

Common visitor to backyard feeders. Listen for their distinctive call.

Observation Calendar

J F M A M J J A S O N D

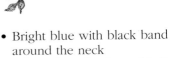

Downy Woodpecker

Picoides pubescens

Size

Habitat

Flying Pattern

- Black crown ends in very bright red spot on back of head
- White extends from cheeks to lower belly
- Wings and tail black with white bands
- Hairy Woodpecker is similar except for a slightly longer bill

DID YOU KNOW?

Can be heard pounding its bill against trees in pursuit of food. Found high up on trunk, moving rapidly from spot to spot. Common visitor to feeders.

Sound

A bright sound *peek...peek*, which may be followed by a rattling call.

Observation Calendar

J F M A M J J A S O N D

Black-capped Chickadee
Parus atricapillus

Size

Habitat

Flying Pattern

Sound

A descending whistle with two notes, *chick-a-dee-dee-dee.*

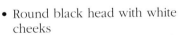

- Round black head with white cheeks
- Black chin contrasts against bright white breast
- Rust along sides and belly
- Wings black and grey with white edges

DID YOU KNOW?

Very curious and will slowly approach you by alighting on nearby branches.

Observation Calendar
J F M A M J J A S O N D

44

American Crow
Corvus brachyrhynchos

Size

Habitat

- Shiny black feathers, with hint of purple
- Large, broad black bill
- Distinguishable from the Raven by its smaller size, thinner bill and squared (rather then diamond-shaped) tail feathers

DID YOU KNOW?

Often seen flying overhead or perched at the top of trees. Acrobatic in flight, even flying upside down, often with other crows.

Flying Pattern

Sound

Various calls, commonest a long nasal *caaaa-a-a*.

Observation Calendar

J F M A M J J A S O N D

45

Red-tailed Hawk
Buteo jamaicensis

Size

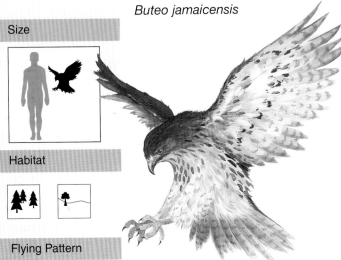

Habitat

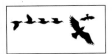

Flying Pattern

- Wings dark brown with buff edges
- Broad white wings and belly, banded with charcoal
- Eyes brick red set against dark brown head
- Tail appears faint red in flight

Sound

A scream that is a downward *keer er er*.

Observation Calendar
J F M A M J J A S O N D

46

Turkey Vulture
Cathartes aura

Size

Habitat

Flying Pattern

Sound

Grunts and hisses when aggressive or feeding.

- Large bird, black overall
- Grey underside of wings is seen in flight
- Featherless red head
- Beak pale yellow, sharply curved

DID YOU KNOW?
Easily identified in flight by V shape formed by wings.

Eastern Bluebird
Sialia sialis

Size

Habitat

Flying Pattern

Sound

Song is bright whistle *cheer cheerful charmer.* Call is lower *turrweee.*

- Upper parts bright blue
- Throat and sides tan
- Belly white
- Female less brilliant, with grey-blue head

Observation Calendar

J F M A M J J A S O N D

48

Red-winged Blackbird

Agelaius phoeniceus

Size

Habitat

Flying Pattern

- Male: black overall with distinctive red shoulder patch
- Female: brown overall with buff eyebrows and chin, chest and belly streaked with darker brown

DID YOU KNOW?

Usually seen at water's edge perched in tall grasses on reeds or other brush.

Sound

Song is *ocalleeee ocaalee.*

Observation Calendar

J F M A M J J A S O N D

49

Great Blue Heron
Ardea herodias

Size

Habitat

Flying Pattern

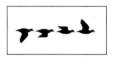

Sound

Bill makes clacking sound. Call is harsh *squawk*.

- Overall grey-blue with black plume on top of head
- Long neck and bill
- Black patch around eyes and extending down long yellow bill
- Long, grey legs

DID YOU KNOW?
Usually spotted standing perfectly still in shallow waters. In flight folds its neck and extends its long legs.

Observation Calendar
J F M A M J J A S O N D

Sharp-shinned Hawk

30 cm / 12 in

- Long, square tail white with charcoal bands
- Wings dark brown
- Top of head dark brown
- Call is a quick, high-pitched *kik kik kik*

Wild Turkey

1.2 m / 4 ft

- Extremely large, body dark brown overall
- Iridescent bronze sheen and banding of red-brown, black and white
- Gobbling and clucking calls

Common Raven

- Shiny, black feathers
- Large, thick, black bill
- Call is a deep resonating *croak*

60 cm / 24 in

Northern Flicker

- Grey crown with bright red spot on back of neck
- Black line runs from bottom of bill along cheek
- Black half-moon "necklace"

30 cm / 12 in

American Robin

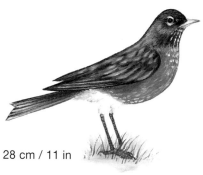

- Back and wings charcoal brown with white edges
- Tail dark grey
- Song is *cheerily cheerily cheerily* in a whistle tone

28 cm / 11 in

Ruby-throated Hummingbird

- Head dark green, iridescent in parts
- Male: red throat, darker under chin
- Call is an occasional chattering or an angry-sounding *squeak*

7.6 cm / 3 in

Purple Martin

- Shiny, dark purple overall
- Female has white front, speckled
- Black bill short, slightly curved
- Call is a high-pitched *cheer cheer*

20 cm / 8 in

Tree Swallow

- Dark iridescent blue, with bright white chin, chest and belly
- Females have brown patch on forehead when mature

15 cm / 6 in

Barn Swallow

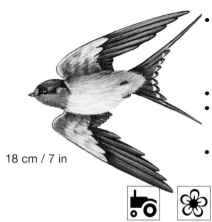

18 cm / 7 in

- Dark blue iridescence from top of head to shoulders, back and top of wings
- Chin, chest rusty
- Wings very long, extending to tips of tail
- Tail long, forked

Scarlet Tanager

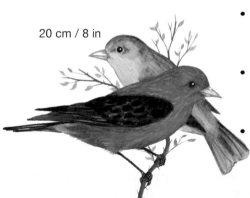

20 cm / 8 in

- Male is scarlet red from head to rump with black wings
- Female is olive-yellow overall with dark wings and tail
- Call is *chip burr*

Northern Cardinal

- Male is brilliant red overall with stout red-orange bill
- Female is buff and grey with hints of bright red on crest
- Song is a series of repeated whistles *wheit cheer cheer cheer*. Also *chip*.

23 cm / 9 in

House Finch

- Male has red crown, chin and chest, buff belly, darker brown back and wings
- Female is grey-brown overall
- Call is a musical warble ending with *jeeeeer*

15 cm / 6 in

Insects & Spiders

Insects are invertebrates, which means that instead of an internal skeleton and backbone, they have a hard coating, called a cuticle. It can be thick and hard for protection, thin and soft for flexibility and even stretchy for movement. It can be permeable to water or gases, or solid and waterproof. The versatility of the cuticle is one of the main reasons that insects are so adaptable and are found in a wide variety of habitats.

There are two main groups: those with wings, such as grasshoppers, and those without, such as silverfish.

An insect's body is divided into three main parts — head, thorax and abdomen. They have two antennae and six legs, all having special organs for sensing sound vibrations and movement and to "taste" and "smell" food. Their eyes let them see fine details and give them good night vision.

Spiders differ from insects in several ways: they have four pairs of legs and two parts to their body, the thorax and abdomen and they have eight eyes. On their abdomen they have two or three pairs of spinnerets with which they spin threads of silk to form nests to protect their eggs and young.

Monarch
Danaus plexippus

Size

Habitat

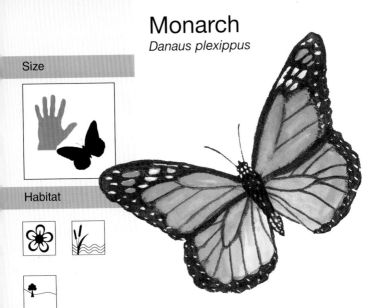

- Large butterfly
- Orange overall with black trim
- Paler orange on underside of wings
- Torso and head black with white speckles

CATERPILLAR
One to 3 broods: July through August.

DID YOU KNOW?
The bright colours of the Monarch warn predators that they are not palatable.

Observation Calendar

J F M A M J J A S O N D

Viceroy
Limenitis archippus

Size

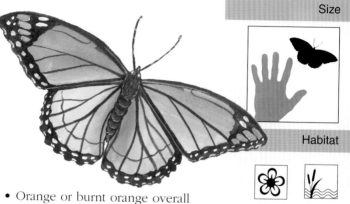

Habitat

- Orange or burnt orange overall with black trim
- Wide black line through middle of each wing
- Underside of wing lighter with distinct black band across
- Body black on back with white speckles on underside

CATERPILLAR
Three broods: early June to late August.

DID YOU KNOW?
It is thought that the Viceroy's colours mimic the Monarch's, sending a warning to birds that they are not palatable.

Observation Calendar

J F M A M J J A S O N D

59

Cabbage White
Pieris rapae

Size

Habitat

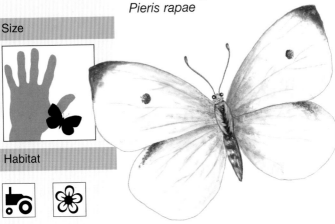

- Dusty white overall with black-tipped wings
- Males have 1 dot on wings, females 2
- Underside of wings are pale yellow-green or greyish

CATERPILLAR

Four or more broods: mid-April to late October.

DID YOU KNOW?

The Cabbage White was introduced to Canada in the 1860s and has since spread to vast regions of the country.

Observation Calendar

J F M A M J J A S O N D

Eastern Tiger Swallowtail

Papilio glaucus

Size

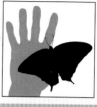

Habitat

- Light yellow overall with black banding across tops of wings
- Hind wings with orange tips and long tails at ends
- Furry body with black on top and yellow on sides
- Yellow spots along edge of wings and wing tips edged in yellow

CATERPILLAR

Two broods: early May to September.

DID YOU KNOW?

This Swallowtail is similar to the Canadian Swallowtail but bigger. There is also a black variety which is believed to mimic the poisonous Pipevine Swallowtail.

Observation Calendar

J F M A M J J A S O N D

Red Admiral
Vanessa atalanta

Size

Habitat

- Dark brown overall with orange and yellow bands
- White markings at tips of forewings
- Underside of wings mottled black, grey and white
- Black spots on orange banding on bottom wing

CATERPILLAR
Three to 4 broods: mid-March to mid-November.

DID YOU KNOW?
The Red Admiral migrates as far south as Guatemala and must recolonize more northern areas each spring.

Observation Calendar
J F M A M J J A S O N D

Orange Sulphur
Colias eurytheme

Size

Habitat

- Soft yellow overall with at least some orange, black edges to wings
- Black dots on upper side of wings appear white on underside
- Furry head with light green eyes
- Female of species has white phase

CATERPILLAR
Four to 7 broods: mid-May to early November.

DID YOU KNOW?
The Orange Sulphur is considered a pest in alfalfa fields.

Observation Calendar

J F M A M J J A S O N D

Eyed Brown
Satyrodes eurydice

Size

Habitat

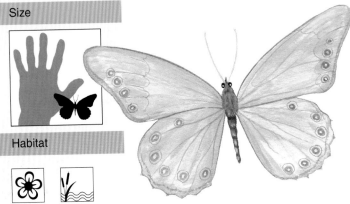

- Light brown overall with distinct eye-shaped circles of black, brown and white
- Antennae with brown and black bands
- Light brown bands through wings
- Bands at ends of wings

CATERPILLAR
One brood: late June to mid-August.

DID YOU KNOW?
This species feeds on sap and may eat bird droppings and rotting fruit as well.

Observation Calendar
J F M A M J J A S O N D

Skippers
Hesperiidae spp.

Size

Habitat

- Stout, furry body with small wings
- Variable colouration mottled in orange, brown, black with some white
- Large eyes

DID YOU KNOW?
Many species occur, too numerous for easy identification. Body length, colour, wing size all vary. Check advanced field guides for detailed notes.

Observation Calendar

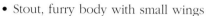

J F M A M J J A S O N D

Great Spangled Fritillary

Speyeria cybele

Size

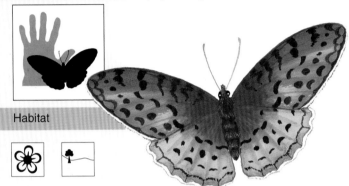

Habitat

- Orange to yellow-orange overall
- Wings brown closer to body, paler on undersides
- Black mottling on wings
- Brown body

CATERPILLAR

One brood: flight season late June to late August.

DID YOU KNOW?

The females scatter their eggs near withered violets in the fall.

Observation Calendar

J F M A M J J A S O N D

Clouded Sulphur
Colias philodice

Size

Habitat

- Dusty yellow overall with small
- Females have white phase
- Often hangs upside down on branches in resting position

CATERPILLAR
Four to 6 broods per season: mid-May to early October.

DID YOU KNOW?
The Clouded, or Common Sulphur is similar to the Orange Sulphur and will occasionally hybridize with them.

Observation Calendar
J F M A M J J A S O N D

Giant Swallowtail

- Large, black wings with yellow markings, light yellow undersides
- 2 small orange dots on back of wings
- Distinct long tails at base of wings
- Hind wing with broad yellow band near base

15 cm / 6 in

Eastern Tailed Blue

- Soft white with soft blue overall
- Wings spotted randomly, with 2 light yellow marks at end of tail

3 cm / 1.25 in

Northern Bluet
Enallagma cyathigerum

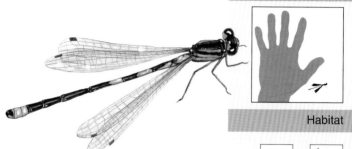

Size

Habitat

- Long, slender body with clear wings
- Blue or occasionally green overall with black on top

DID YOU KNOW?
This is one of the few animals that we may commonly watch mate and lay eggs. The acrobatic "wheel position" of a mating pair is familiar to many of us.

Size

Habitat

Sound

Movement of wings and legs makes buzzing sound.

Spur-throated Grasshopper
Schistocera americana

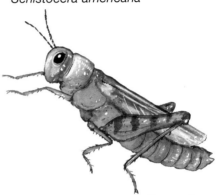

- Brown to green overall
- Short antennae about 1/3 body length
- Strong jumping legs with black bands and small spurs
- Wings yellow with black edges

DID YOU KNOW?

Can eat up to 10 times its weight each day, which causes problems in farming communities.

Observation Calendar

J F M A M J J A S O N D

Honey Bee
Apus mellifera

Size

Habitat

- Dark overall with yellow bands along abdomen
- Smoky wings fold back over abdomen
- Hairy legs will often have a large globule of collected pollen attached

Sound

Familiar *buzz* when in flight.

Observation Calendar
J F M A M J J A S O N D

71

Dragonfly
Cordulegaster spp.

Size

Habitat

- Very large with varying colours, commonly yellow and black
- Large bulging eyes at sides of head

DID YOU KNOW?
Commonly seen along edges of grassy area near water.

Observation Calendar
J F M A M J J A S O N D

72

Deer Fly
Chrysops spp.

Size

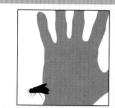

Habitat

- Dark overall with short antennae
- Wings smoky with black patches
- Can inflict painful bite

Sound

Faint *buzz* when flying.

DID YOU KNOW?
Try not to wave your arms too much at a nearby Deer Fly, as they are attracted to movement.

Observation Calendar
J F M A M J J A S O N D

73

Bumble Bee
Bombus terrestris

Size

Habitat

Sound

Faint *buzz* in flight.

- Furry with black and yellow markings
- Brown wings fold back over body
- Short antennae
- Large round body — more rotund than Honey Bee

Observation Calendar
J F M A M J J A S O N D

74

Wolf Spider
Lycosa spp.

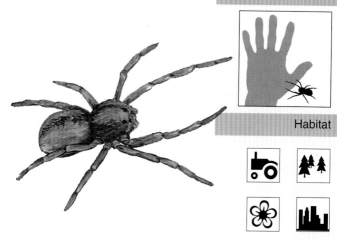

Size

Habitat

- Large, with light and dark brown coloration
- Occasionally you will see a female carrying young on her back

DID YOU KNOW?

The presence of Wolf Spiders is marked by their webs found in short grass.

Daddy Long Legs
Leiobunum rotundum

Size

Habitat

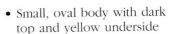

- Small, oval body with dark top and yellow underside
- Long, thin, delicate legs
- Does not bite
- Moves slowly over ground

Observation Calendar
J F M A M J J A S O N D

Lightning Bug
Photuris pennsylvanica

Size

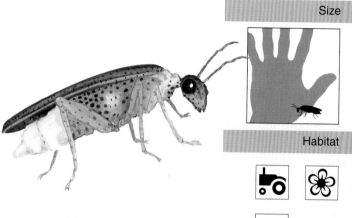

Habitat

- Red shoulders and upper body, black torso with long dark wings
- Torso glows at dusk and nightfall, from chemical process

DID YOU KNOW?
Swarms of Lightning Bugs, also known as Fireflies, can be seen in open fields at dusk.

Observation Calendar
J F M A M J J A S O N D

Two-spotted Ladybird Beetle
Adalia bipunctata

Size

Habitat

- Oval body, dark red with spots on either side
- Black head with white spotting

DID YOU KNOW?
Large swarms can be seen in September, but mostly Ladybirds are solitary insects often found on the lower branches of bushes.

Observation Calendar
J F M A M J J A S O N D

78

Mosquito

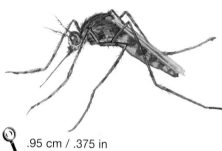

- Brown and grey overall with wings folded back
- Long slender legs and proboscis
- Makes a faint *buzz* in flight

 .95 cm / .375 in

Black Fly

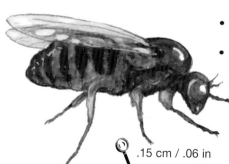

- Tiny, black overall
- Small head bent down, humpbacked

 .15 cm / .06 in

79

American House Spider

- Mottled yellow and brown
- Long, slender legs with spurs
- Females larger of species, with large swollen abdomens

1.3 cm / 0.5 in

Female

Male

Buffalo Treehopper

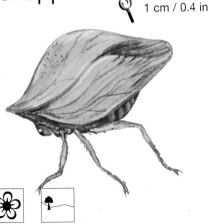

1 cm / 0.4 in

- Stout, bright green to yellow body shaped like a buffalo head
- Clear wings taper toward abdomen

80

Field Cricket

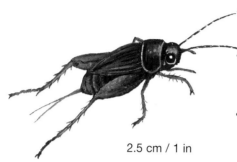

- Shiny brown or black body, slightly flat
- Long threadlike antennae, protruding forward
- Transparent wings are usually folded back over body

2.5 cm / 1 in

True Katydid

6 cm / 2.5 in

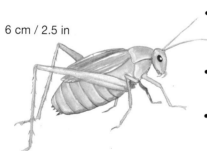

- Light green, occasionally brown, mimicking a leaf
- Thick body, forewings, pointed head
- Makes a 2-part *katy-DID* sound, sometimes repeated

Tiger Beetle

- Iridescent blue and green with long slender body
- Occasionally has small spots
- Very fast-moving

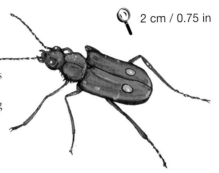 2 cm / 0.75 in

    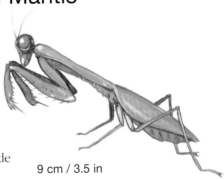

European Mantis

- Long green or brown body, long neck and small head
- Front legs like vice-grips with claws for clutching prey
- Can turn head from side to side

9 cm / 3.5 in

Paper Wasp

- Black with markings of yellow and reddish brown
- Smoky wings extend past abdomen
- Makes a faint *buzzing* in flight

2.5 cm / 1 in

Yellow Jacket

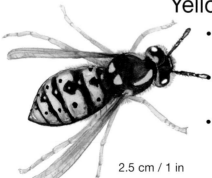

- Distinctive yellow and black markings
- Narrow "waist" between thorax and abdomen
- Makes a faint *buzzing* in flight

2.5 cm / 1 in

Crane Fly

- Thin body and head
- Dark brown legs twice as long as body

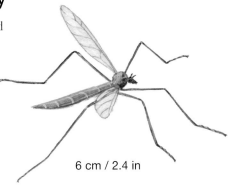

6 cm / 2.4 in

Water Strider

- Long, dark brown body with small water repellent hairs, white underside
- Front legs short, back legs extremely long

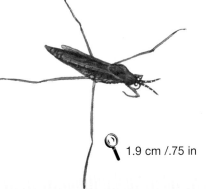

1.9 cm / .75 in

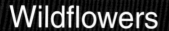

Wildflowers

When identifying plants in the wild you will be looking at the leaf and the blossom. The shape of the leaf and the stem, the number of petals and their colour are all important clues. Most flowers bloom for only a few weeks each summer, but you will find that if you have identified the flower once, then when you find the plant in the fall, you will have no difficulty identifying it. The observation calendar shows when it blooms.

Wildflowers in their habitat make beautiful photographs. It is a more "natural" way to enjoy them than by picking them and taking them home. Besides, wildflowers don't last very long in a vase. The species included here are among the most prolific in southwest Ontario.

Buttercup
Ranunculus spp.

Size

Habitat

Alternate Name

Crowfoot

- Five waxy, yellow petals with yellow centre
- Grows in clusters close to ground
- Leaves serrated, similar to a maple leaf

DID YOU KNOW?
Buttercup is food for waterfowl and game birds such as pheasants.

Observation Calendar
J F M A M J J A S O N D

Swamp Milkweed

Asclepias incarnata

Size

Habitat

- Light purple–rose flowers
- Thick stalks support 18 pairs of large, smooth leaves which curve upward
- Seed pods are large with rough skin; contain hairy, silky seeds

DID YOU KNOW?

Milkweed is a food source for muskrats and Monarch Butterflies. Young shoots and pods can be added to soups and other cooked dishes. White juice in seed pods can be irritating if in contact with eyes.

Observation Calendar

J F M A M J J A S O N D

Starflower
Trientalis borealis

- Star-shaped white flowers, usually one to three per plant
- 6 to 7 pointed, white petals
- Broad, shiny leaves with deep veins
- Flowers at top of short stems with leaves spreading out in fan shape

Observation Calendar
J F M A M J J A S O N D

Yellow Goat's Beard
Tragopogon dubius

Size

Habitat

- Solitary flower yellow with several pointed petals and yellow centre
- Flower head is nestled in a row of long, spiky, green petals
- Flower head in seed is round, white, similar to dandelion

DID YOU KNOW?
Roots can be used in cooking. Young plant leaves and lower mature leaves can be used as cooked vegetable or in salads.

Observation Calendar

J F M A M J J A S O N D

89

Blue Flag
Iris versicolor

Size

Habitat

Alternate Name

Harlequin Blueflag

- Large, single flower with wide, purple petals turning yellow toward centre
- Spike-like leaves taper to point
- Leaves grow from individual stems
- Plants grow in small clusters

DID YOU KNOW?
All parts are poisonous.

Observation Calendar
J F M A M J J A S O N D

90

Goldenrod
Solidago spp.

Size

Habitat

- Flower heads are elongated clusters of yellow florets
- Long, thin leaves taper to a point
- Large, bushy plant
- Grows in large groups

DID YOU KNOW?

Young leaves can be used as greens in salads. Flowers can be dried and used for teas.

Observation Calendar

J F M A M J J A S O N D

91

Ox-eye Daisy
Chrysanthemum leucanthemum

Size

Habitat

- Solitary flower has many narrow white petals and a yellow centre
- Leaves are wavy, deeply lobed, tapering to a point and clasped around stem at base
- Numerous stems rise from base
- Leaves are smaller near flower

DID YOU KNOW?
The Ox-eye Daisy's young leaves can be used in salads.

Observation Calendar
J F M A M J J A S O N D

Dark-eyed Susan
Rudbeckia hirta

Size

Habitat

- Bright orange-yellow petals surround a dark brown centre, daisy-like
- Single, bristly stalk
- Leaves serrated, tapering to a point

DID YOU KNOW?
Takes 2 seasons to bloom. Bitter taste.

Observation Calendar
J F M A M J J A S O N D

Queen Anne's Lace
Daucus carota

Size

Habitat

Alternate Name

Wild Carrot

- White 5-petalled florets grow in flat, dome-shaped clusters
- Tiny purple flower in centre of cluster
- Leaves and stem hairy

DID YOU KNOW?
Roots are edible but are considered poisonous in older plants. Seeds are eaten by warblers and other small birds and mice.

Observation Calendar
J F M A M J J A S O N D

Canada Thistle
Cirsium arvense

Size

Habitat

 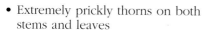

- Extremely prickly thorns on both stems and leaves
- Flower purplish-pink, occasionally white
- Several layers of thorny leaves surround flower head

DID YOU KNOW?
Leaves and stalk can be used in salads or cooked after thorns and outer layer of stem are removed. Best to cook with young plants.

Observation Calendar
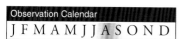
J F M A M J J A S O N D

Marsh Marigold
Caltha palustris

Size

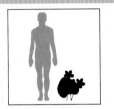

Habitat

- Small, yellow 5-petalled flower with yellow centre
- Grows in clusters, forming ground cover
- Broad, light green, kidney-shaped leaves with serrated edges

DID YOU KNOW?
Flower buds can be pickled. Young leaves can be boiled and eaten.

Observation Calendar
J F M A M J J A S O N D

Bloodroot
Sanguinaria canadensis

Size

Habitat

Alternate Names

Indian Paint
Red Root
Tetterwort

- White flower, cupped with about 8 petals, yellow centre
- Large lobed leaf, dark green, encircles stalk
- Poisonous red sap in root
- Gold stamen

Observation Calendar
J F M A M J J A S O N D

Purple Loosestrife

- 6-petalled, magenta flowers
- Flowers cluster on long tapering stems
- Thick individual stems grow in groups

1.2 m / 4ft

Evening Primrose

- 4 yellow petals with yellow centre
- Opens in evening and closes by morning
- Leaves with hairs, alternate, tapering to points

15 cm / 6 in

Blue Aster

60 cm / 24 in

- Several light purple petals, yellow centre
- Bushy with many stems
- Non-serrated leaves taper to point

Cow Parsnip

1.2 m / 4 ft

- White, 5-petalled flowers grow in clusters
- Shape of cluster similar to Queen Anne's Lace
- Large leaves in 3 main sections, similar to maple leaf

Stinking Chamomile

- Daisy-like, with yellow centre
- White petals usually curve downward but often will be random
- Sturdy branched stem, thin leaves
- Grows in groups

30 cm / 12 in

Flat-topped Aster

- Slender with white petals, yellow centres
- Flowers at ends of clustered stems
- Oval leaves with smooth tapering edges

60 cm / 24 in

Ragwort

- Several yellow flower heads together in flat-topped clusters
- Yellow petals and centres
- Deeply cut leaves, alternate along stem
- Bush-like plant

2 m / 6 ft

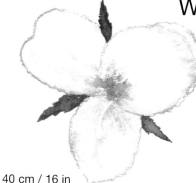

White Trillium

- 3-petal flower with yellow centre
- Grow in colonies in shaded areas
- Flowers gain pink tint over time
- Ontario's provincial floral emblem

40 cm / 16 in

Rue Anemone

- White flower with 5 petals on short stalk
- Centre of flower pale yellow
- Grows in groups on forest floor

13 cm / 5 in

Tufted Vetch

- Numerous purple flowers grow together on one side of stalk
- Vine-like plant intertwines with other plants
- Many leaflets lining stem help to climb

60 cm / 24 in

Blackberry

125 cm / 50 in

- 5-petalled white flowers with light green centre
- Flowers grow in small clusters on very hard, thorny stems
- Leaves serrated, tapering to point, similar to raspberry

Yellow Rocket

60 cm / 24 in

- Clusters of tiny florets
- Flowers have 4 yellow petals, darker yellow centres
- Upper leaves are serrated and oval

103

Fragrant Water Lily

- Aquatic plant with white or pinkish petals and yellow centre
- Large, round, shiny dark green leaves float on surface

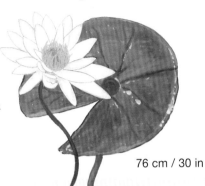

76 cm / 30 in

Wild Strawberry

- 5 round white petals with yellow centre
- Short, hairy stalk
- Leaves deeply serrated, grow in groups of 3
- Grows close to the ground

18 cm / 7 in

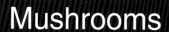

Mushrooms

Mushrooms are some of the most exotic and appealing plants that grow in the wild. They are the fruits of fungus that grow as threadlike fibres in the soil. The mushroom's function is to produce spores. These are the "seeds" which then propagate the fungus by being carried by animals or insects or by wind or water. Some mushrooms produce spores on gills, some on teeth and some inside a leathery pouch, like the puffballs. The morels produce them inside a shallow cup.

There are many species of mushrooms and it is very important to bear in mind that the edible ones can easily be confused with the poisonous ones. It is not advisable to pick mushrooms, or other fungi, at any time in the wild. Like wildflowers, they make very good subjects for nature photography.

Many people can recognize gilled mushrooms. They are typically parasol-shaped and have blade-like gills on the underside and stems with or without rings. Pore mushrooms are similar but have a spongy layer of tubes on the underside of the cap. The following species will help you appreciate some of the treasures to be found on the forest floor and in open meadows in spring and fall.

Pigskin Poison Puffball

- Several varieties
- Small, round and delicate, chalky white

Destroying Angel

- Tall white stem with thin cap
- Cap convex and sometimes flat

Birch Polypore

- Large white disc found only on birch trees
- Brown mottling on edge near tree

106

Dead Man's Fingers

- White in spring, turning black at maturity
- Grows near base of rotting stumps

Turkey Tail

- Resembles wild turkey tail-feathers spread apart
- Grows in clumps on decaying trees

Fawn Mushroom

- Cap dark brown, smooth
- Stalk white

Fly Agaric

- Cap bright red with white bumps
- Stalk white

King Bolete

- Giant cap 25 cm (10 in) across, brownish
- Stalk wide, white with veins

Common Scaber Stalk

- Cap 15 cm (6 in) across, light brown
- Stalk white with grey speckles

Trees

Trees and shrubs grow well in southwest
Ontario. There are many imported species
as well as native ones in parks and on land
that has returned to wilderness. A tree is identified
by the shape and colour of the leaf, the texture of
the bark, the overall shape of the tree, and its size.

Trees are vital to the life of the planet because
they help cleanse the air of carbon dioxide They are
essential to most ecosystems by providing shelter
and food for birds, mammals and insects, as well as
being dependent on various organisms, including
insects and other plants, for their survival. A healthy
forest is the result of a balance of many different life
forms. Forestry practices, urban sprawl and road
construction wilfully destroy trees with heavy
machinery. Replanting takes place in small
numbers, but the birds, animals and
insects, as well as all the smaller plants
that create the ecosystem have all been
displaced or destroyed along with
the trees.

Understanding the variety and value
of trees in the landscape will be enhanced
by being able to identify some of the
common species included in this book.

Sugar Maple
Acer saccharum

Size

Habitat

Fall Colour

- Straight and tall with more branch branch development when growing in open areas
- Leaf is dull green with small hairs on paler bottom
- Bark is grey, smooth with ridges

FLOWER
Long reddish clusters in early spring.

FRUIT
Key 2.5 cm (1 in) long, wing-like, red turning red-brown.

FOOD
Deer feed on the branches and several birds and small mammals feed on the seeds.

DID YOU KNOW?
The Sugar Maple leaf is depicted on the Canadian flag.

Red Maple
Acer rubrum

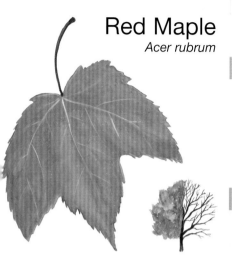

Size

Habitat

Fall Colour

- Very large tree with broad growth, compact limbs
- Leaves dull green with veins, serrated edge
- Bark, thin, grey, smooth with ridges

FLOWER
Clusters of tiny, light-red flowers in early spring.

FRUIT
Small key, or "propeller," with wings, light green turning red-brown.

DID YOU KNOW?
In the 1800s, Canadians made ink and dyes from bark extract.

Manitoba Maple
Acer negundo

Size

Habitat

- Medium size overall with short trunk and broad crown
- Bark light brown-grey with narrow, sometimes deep ridges

FLOWER
Small clusters of light purple flowers appear before the leaves in spring.

FRUIT
Double keys with wings.

FOOD
Once harvested for its sap. Seeds feed a variety of small mammals and birds.

Fall Colour

DID YOU KNOW?
The Manitoba Maple's distinguishing feature is the compound leaves growing evenly down both sides of the stem.

Alternate Names

Ashleaf Maple
Boxelder

Tamarack
Larix laricina

Size

Habitat

Alternate Name

American Larch

- Thin trunk with branches reaching out with slight curve
- Deciduous needles, in spring bright green, turning duller green, and bright yellow in fall before falling off
- Bark is red-brown or grey with scales
- Twigs turn orange-brown and later light grey in maturity

FRUIT
Light brown oval cones.

DID YOU KNOW?
The Tamarack is one of the northernmost trees and will survive in extremely cold climates.

113

Pussy Willow
Salix discolor

Size

Habitat

Fall Colour

- Rounded overall, bushy with many stems
- Leaves long, shiny, dark green, serrated and pointed
- Bark dark grey and smooth

FLOWER
Small, soft clusters become furry tufts at maturity.

FOOD
Feeds Ruffed Grouse, Beaver, Muskrat, Red Squirrel and Snowshoe Hare.

DID YOU KNOW?
The Pussy Willow provides a valuable nesting site for many small songbirds including the American Goldfinch.

American Mountain Ash

Sorbus americana

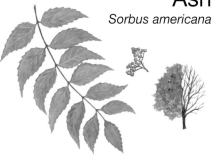

- Leaflets are long, serrated and pointed
- Bushy tree with spreading crown, many stems
- Bark smooth, red-brown and scaly

FLOWER

Small white flowers in flat-topped clusters in May and June.

FRUIT

Orange berries in clumps in late August and September.

FOOD

Feeds Ruffed Grouse, Grey Catbird, Eastern Bluebird, European Starling, Common Grackle, Cedar Waxwing, Grosbeak, Beaver, and Snowshoe Hare.

DID YOU KNOW?

Used chiefly as an ornamental tree in gardens.

Size

Habitat

Fall Colour

White Pine
Pinus strobus

- Tall evergreen with straight trunk and horizontal branches
- Needles soft, bluish long, in bunches of 5
- Bark dark brown, rough
- Diameter of trunk can reach 1.3 m

FRUIT
Cones yellow-brown, narrow.

FOOD
Feeds Junco, Black-capped Chickadee, Boreal Chickadee, Crossbills and many other small birds. Red Squirrel and Chipmunk also feed on seeds.

DID YOU KNOW?
The largest conifer in the northeast, the White Pine is prized for its straight trunk and high-quality lumber.

Flowering Dogwood
Cornus florida

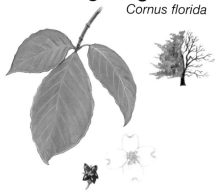

Size

Habitat

Fall Colour

- Small tree with short trunk, branches spreading out widely
- Leaves green with paler underside
- Bark dark red-brown, rough and broken up into sections

FLOWER

Small clusters of white flowers.

FRUIT

Very small red berries.

DID YOU KNOW?

Flowering Dogwood is a valuable material for making jewellers' equipment including blocks and mallet heads, also used to make pulleys.

Staghorn Sumac
Rhus typhina

Size

Habitat

Fall Colour

- Spreading branches from flat, open crown
- Flowers green in spring
- Leaves paired on axis eight to each side, with one at end
- Bark smooth grey-brown

FLOWER
Small green flowers.

FRUIT
Bright red berries grow in clusters.

FOOD
Feeds Ruffed Grouse, Ring-necked Pheasant, Common Crow, Thrushes, American Robin, Eastern Bluebird, European Starling and many other species.

Black Cherry
Prunus serotina

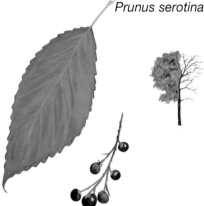

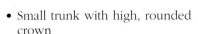

Size

Habitat

- Small trunk with high, rounded crown
- Very aromatic with blossoming flowers and edible fruit
- Leaves shiny, dark green, elliptical with fine serrated edges
- Bark dark brown with red-brown exposed between cracks

Fall Colour

FLOWER
Flowers with 5 round white petals.

FOOD
Feeds a variety of birds and small mammals, as well as humans.

DID YOU KNOW?
Cough medicine and wild cherry syrup are derived from the bark.

Smooth Sumac

- Small bushy tree with stout spreading branches
- Bark brown or grey, smooth with some scales
- Fruit is dark red, covered in sticky hairs

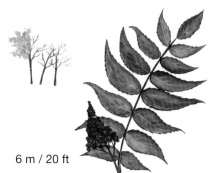

6 m / 20 ft

Paper Birch

- Narrow trunk, splitting into multiple stems
- Thin, papery bark, chalky white with tan highlights
- Wide, dull green leaf, serrated edge, tapering to point

21 m / 70 ft

Northern Red Oak

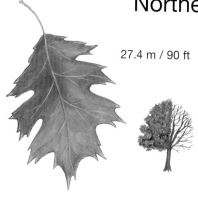

27.4 m / 90 ft

- Large tree with many thick, firm branches
- Underside of leaves, paler, light hairs near veins
- Bark is dark grey-brown, rough with reddish inner bark

Balsam Fir

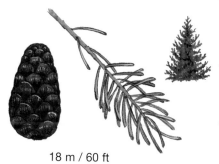

18 m / 60 ft

- Tall evergreen with irregular shape
- Brown bark smooth with resin visible in blisters
- Dark purple, cylindrical cones turn brown

White Spruce

- Tall, straight trunk with horizontal branches hanging slightly downward
- Grey-brown bark smooth with some cuts
- Shiny, light brown cylindrical cones

30.5 m / 100 ft

American Beech

- Large tree with wide spreading branches and rounded top
- Foliage on young trees remains in winter
- Brown burs with prickles that break open in fall

24 m / 80 ft

Red-osier Dogwood

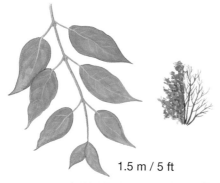

- Large spreading shrub
- Bark's flat plates red-brown or red-grey
- Fruit are white berries

1.5 m / 5 ft

White Ash

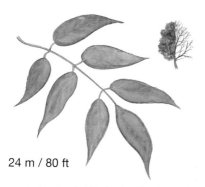

- Large, slender tree, dense branches
- Leaves dark green, with smooth edge and point at end
- Small purple flowers grow in clusters

24 m / 80 ft

Black Willow

- Large with several trunks, vertical or leaning slightly
- Bark dark brown or blackish, deep ridges
- Fruit are small, elongated, red-brown catkins

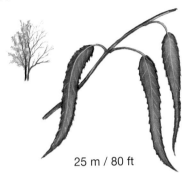

25 m / 80 ft

Yellow Birch

- Large, oval-shaped tree with drooping branches
- Bark shiny, light yellow, thin papery layers
- Flowers are light yellow with drooping catkins at end of twigs

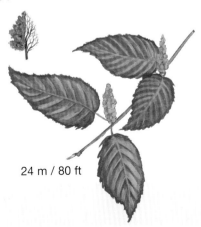

24 m / 80 ft

White Oak

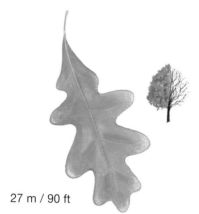

27 m / 90 ft

- Dense, wide-spreading branches
- Bark light grey with ridges forming plates
- Small acorns, cap on top turning light grey

Black Oak

21 m / 70 ft

- Widely spread branches stretching upward
- Bark grey and smooth with ridges
- Acorns long, thin, topped with cap

Index

By the same author:

Lorimer's Pocketguides, written and illustrated by Jeffrey C. Domm, are designed for readers of all ages who want handy-sized reference books to birds in their area. Each book has 120 original, full-colour illustrations that show the identifying marks of commonly seen species. They are accompanied by brief descriptions and visual keys to show size and habitat. A two-step bird finder allows readers to use the book as a quick and easy reference.

Each book provides a list and a map of the best birding hotspots in and around each city. These were compiled by local birding experts.

Jeffrey Domm's reputation as a wildlife artist is growing across North America. He has created posters and educational materials for Parks Canada, Fisheries and Oceans Canada and Environment Canada and he has had shows of his wildlife art in New York and Nova Scotia.

The Lorimer Pocketguide to Hamilton Birds
The Lorimer Pocketguide to Kitchener-Waterloo Birds
The Lorimer Pocketguide to London Birds
The Lorimer Pocketguide to Toronto Birds

"… an excellent job. It is certain to be enjoyed by anyone with an interest in birding."
— *Gord Mcnulty, Hamilton Spectator*